OPEN
KITCHENS

BEVERLY MASSACHUSETTS

ROCKPORT
PUBLISHERS

Copyright © 2007 by **LOFT Publications**

First published in the United States of America by
Rockport Publishers, a member of
Quayside Publishing Group
100 Cummings Center
Suite 406-L
Beverly, MA 01915-6101
Telephone: (978) 282-9590
Fax: (978) 283-2742
www.rockpub.com

ISBN-13: 978-1-59253-378-7
ISBN-10: 1-59253-378-7

Editors:
Beate Küper and Montse Borràs

Art Director:
Mireia Casanovas Soley

Layout:
Ignasi Gracia Blanco

Editorial project:
© 2007 **LOFT Publications**
Via Laietana 32, 4th Of. 92.
08003 Barcelona, Spain
Tel.: +34 932 688 088
Fax: +34 932 687 073
loft@loftpublications.com
www.loftpublications.com

Printed in China

Contents

INTRODUCTION

Since antiquity, the *hearth* has been regarded as a synonym for *home*. Over the course of time, man's living space evolved around this place. It represented the center for routine domestic tasks as well as a place for storytelling, where people would gather to exchange information and enjoy the warmth of the fire. Ever since, the kitchen has been considered the heart of the home.

Accordingly, the contemporary kitchen has many different functions. Unlike most other spaces of the house, demands on this focal point highly depend on the available space and the household structure. Kitchen equipment has always changed according to the different needs and the kitchen has become more and more the center of human social life. This can be found in the expression of "kitchen living." Increasingly, traditional homes, modern studios, and lofts follow the American model of the open kitchen, providing easy access from all sides. Instead of fully fitted features, the trend tends to favor turning flexible elements into real design objects (such as the ventilation hood over the cooking space). Kitchen equipment is increasingly more concealed, as the kitchen becomes the owner's personal showpiece. On the other hand, the dining room recedes in importance, boundaries are eliminated, and rooms gradually merge into one single space.

With modern equipment and ventilation systems that prevent cooking odors from invading the adjacent living space, the popularity of open kitchen spaces has increased even more. Another advantage is the space-saving aspect. Functionality and aesthetics combine to form a new and integrated whole in an open kitchen space. Thus, the kitchen can be seen as one of the best indicators of current trends. The open kitchen stands for an era in which people have a desire for flexibility. In this respect, aesthetics and mobility play an ever-increasing role.

For architects and designers alike, new kitchens have become a growing challenge, where different techniques and factors must come together in one single living area. The intention of this book is to provide inspiration and exploration of the infinite possibilities of open kitchen design.

The main concept of this kitchen was to create a modern space and make it appear as large as possible. This impression comes from the clever floor plan and is enhanced by the integrated mirrors reflecting the interior and the outer garden. The cooking and dining areas merge into one homogeneous space that opens to the garden. The brightly colored seats as well as the other furnishings were designed especially for this kitchen; they harmonize in color and complement the sense of homogeneity. They contrast with the colorful walls that convey a sense of friendliness and vividness, but despite the gaudy colors it is this contrast that creates a harmonious and balanced atmosphere. With these qualities, it is quite obvious that this unique and eye-catching kitchen will not only be used for cooking and dining, but also as the apartment's primary or social meeting space.

HIGHGATE HOUSE

Architect: Jonathan Clark Architects Photos: © Narrative

The soft cream tone chosen as the color for the dining area acts as a focal point, and just behind, the wall has been covered with panels of colors combined to re-create the garden and produce an effect that is both cheerful and relaxing.

The mirrored wall efficiently carries out the function of separating the kitchen from the rest of the house, leaving the stairs clear, which lead to the hall. The most innovative feature, however, is the effect of multiplying both the space and light coming from the garden.

The house, raised on pillars, is situated in the heart of San Diego, California in the middle of a small eucalyptus plantation. Like the trees that surround it, its four semifloors lie on the edge of a canyon, giving one side of the house amazing views. The arrangement of the many windows and glass doors allows the garden and the vegetation to penetrate the rooms.

The kitchen, in the narrowest part of the house, especially benefits from this position, receiving light from the garden on one side, and from the other the light that penetrates through the treetops from the raised windows on the east side. The stainless steel work surfaces have been posi-

tioned parallel to the lower windows in order to take advantage of the natural light and to be able to enjoy the garden. In the center, dividing the work space from the dining area, there is an island whose surface is a slab of slate, in sharp contrast with the finishes of the rest of the cedar furniture, whose fluting creates an organic effect in keeping with the house's surroundings.

The exterior wall has been opened in such as way that it connects the room with the garden and a customized cage has been created from stainless steel netting for the house pet, a blue and golden macaw.

LOMAC RESIDENCE (TREE HOUSE)

Architect: Safdie Rabines Architects Photos: © Undine Pröhl

The owners of this house, a young dynamic couple, wanted a space that would allow them to create an intimate setting that would allow for both informal and formal gatherings.

This was an old Victorian house with a long, narrow floor plan, divided into different rooms. The space for the kitchen is on the lower floor and is the true nucleus of this area, either side of which two rooms have been added, one for rest and the other for eating. A more conventional dining room is situated to one side of the kitchen, in the old part of the house, with a classic sturdy wooden table. On the other side is an informal lounge next to the terrace, which also has its own more casual dining area. This interior terrace is a strong element, because it gives impulse to the flow created by the successive open spaces, which carry out different social roles. The different levels of the house have been turned into an advantage, since a single continual space is divided into various progressive modules: living room-dining room-kitchen-lounge-terrace.

Light is an element that gives this project personality, because a lighting system has been created that allows for up to ten different scenarios, creating atmospheres that are intimate or festive depending on the mood, and which lights the kitchen with powerful and efficient spotlights in order to work comfortably. A fine beam of light illuminates the floor parallel to the exterior wall, showing the transition in level that separates the dining room from the kitchen.

For the floor, a simple white polished concrete was chosen that has both a contemporary and elegant feel.

VIEW STREET HOUSE

Architect: Andy Macdonald/Mac-Interactive Photos: © Murray Fredericks

The interior lighting effect, which has been carried out parallel to the architectural work both in the kitchen and living area and the back terrace, can be appreciated from the outside. The metal framework provides intimacy and acts as a formal complement to the façade.

The stairs that lead to the upper flat start at the area dividing the kitchen and living spaces. The ebony polished wooden steps enhance the chromatic and functional contrast between these two rooms and heighten communication between the different areas of the house.

Plan

This 2,368 sq ft (220 sq meter) open-plan space, posed the problem of having all the windows on one side, which created an imbalance towards this single source of light. This determined the positioning of all the main spaces by the windows, leaving those spaces with less need of natural light on the west side.

Following these parameters, the walls that were put up did not reach the ceiling. Glass strips were built for the upper sections to allow the light to reach every corner of the house. The kitchen, situated at the side has less light and reaps the benefits of this solution. A cubicle has been built, which integrates the electrical appliances and other elements from the kitchen, leaving the sink in the central island, which contains the dishwasher. The area behind this island can becomes a small bar by using high stools there.

The surfaces have been clad in white marble, thereby favoring the range of light colors that has been chosen here. The communication between the kitchen and living room is through the dining area, which is situated between the two and benefits from the direct light from the windows. This way a highly functional flow is created between the three spaces.

The wall at the back of the kitchen has been covered in a mosaic of blue tones, indicating the work area in a discreet, careful, and original way. In conjunction with this, the modular furniture in the kitchen is covered in panels of a neutral shade of green, which elegantly harmonizes with the stainless steel in the electrical appliances and in some of the finishes.

The dining area, where white dominates, stands out by virtue of its proximity to the living area and its eye-catching black sofa.

HUDSON STREET LOFT

Architect: Moneo Brock Studio Photos: © Jordi Miralles

Plan

This is an example of how solar energy in private homes can be synonymous with beauty and elegance. This house, in a tranquil and exclusive area of Vienna, is situated on a steeply inclined site surrounded by woodlands. The idea was to make the three stories as openplan and as full of light as possible. Glass therefore became one of the essential materials in the construction. Natural light reaches the ground floor directly via a system of skylights.

The kitchen is on the ground floor, above the basement, together with the living room, the dining area, and the library with a large panel of shelving that covers the central wall of this floor. The entire floor, including the kitchen, is made from different shades of gray polished stone, in keeping with the concrete walls. The kitchen has been strategically positioned behind the stairs,

so that although it has a fluid connection with the other spaces, it is kept slightly apart, behind a panel of glass. This way, it receives all the light from the outside and the other spaces are protected from cooking odors. The central wall that rises from the basement has been used to finish the countertop in the kitchen, and a glass panel has been mounted on it, parallel to the stair banisters that pass behind.

In the kitchen, concrete is the main element, and the modules and electrical appliances are all finished in stainless steel. On the ceiling, three parallel fluorescent tubes, serve as extra lighting.

One of the main features of this house is the generosity of the spaces. The perception of space is further enhanced by the amount of glass that seemingly allows the outdoor vegetation to penetrate the interior and conversely makes the floor seem to continue into the forest.

SOLAR TUBE

Architect: Georg Driendl/Driendl Architects   Photos: © Bruno Klomfar

The ingenious layout of this plan and how this interior space has been opened to the exterior light can be appreciated from the hallway. There is totally fluid communication between the different spaces without disregarding the clear borders between them.

The wooden steps, fixed to the glass, appear to be floating in front of the kitchen, thus creating a new and intermittent visual separation. The classic wall opposite the work surface has been avoided, providing light.

The splendid views that this coastal house north of Barcelona provides were a deciding factor in opening up the living areas as much as possible to the outside.

The fundamental concept in terms of the layout of the spaces is an attempt to encourage the communication flow. This is why the kitchen is delineated intermittently by way of one of the project's distinctive concepts. The "furniture architecture," turns architectural units into pieces of furniture, thereby increasing their functionality. Thus the intermittent "walls" that separate the kitchen from the hall area are cupboards and shelves; likewise a camouflaged storage space has been incorporated in the stairwell, which also acts as a dividing feature.

The selection of materials and colors plays a fundamental role in the different spaces offering coherence to the continuity and highlighting the functions in each one. The vivid red of the columns/cupboard, made from DM, stands out against the thickness and warmth of the oak in the flooring throughout the house. The central island that integrates the key functions of the kitchen is also built from oak, although in this case it has been stained chocolate brown. On top of this, another parallel volume has been installed that contains the ventilation hood and the lighting for the countertop. The cupboard handles match the matt stainless steel edging. The surface of the table and the countertop have been custom designed from white Silestone, giving continuity to the white walls and the white façades.

HOUSE IN CABRERA

Architect: Ramon Pintó   Photos: © Jordi Miralles

This open kitchen is located inside a 3,229 sq ft (300 sq meter) penthouse that belongs to two art collectors. It connects to the dining room that again opens to the spacious living room just around the corner. This structure creates a very open character that is further enhanced by the large windows. The kitchen consists mainly of a large island that incorporates all necessary appliances and fixtures. Additional storage space can be found in the large cupboards on the wall. The simple forms and white surfaces form a contrast to the colorful art collection that decorates the entire apartment and creates a bright and friendly atmosphere. The kitchen's special feature is the geometric constellation of unfolding transparent wood slats on the ceiling at the end of the kitchen island. This device may be lowered or raised as required. When retracted, it serves as an interesting ceiling sculpture—when lowered, it separates the kitchen from the remaining area without disrupting the space's open character.

CHISWICK PENTHOUSE APARTMENT

Architect: Scape Architects Photos: © Kilian O'Sullivan

The kitchen is integrated into the main body of the apartment, freely receiving all the natural light that arrives from the panels of the large windows. The retractable divider that hangs from the ceiling separates the two rooms, allowing the space to flow freely.

Behind the kitchen, and its minimalist lines, a large panel has been built into the wall with cupboards that contain utensils. In the central island, the sink and cooktop in opposite positions free up more work space. Spotlights under the mezzanine light the space.

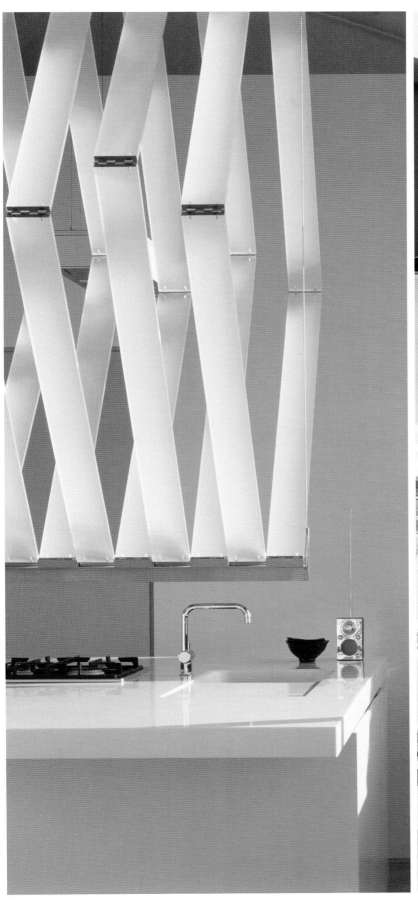

This apartment is part of a massive renovation of an old six-story warehouse situated next to New York's SOHO, parallel to which a modern building of lofts was added. The apartment is on the top floor of the old construction and standing out in this transformation is the innovative kitchen with its eminently urban spirit.

Behind the central module that separates the work area, is a short platform whose hydraulic, easy-clean surface forms a contrast with the dark wood of the rest of the apartment. At one end, a large cupboard has been built in yellow, translucent laminate, which takes up the entire wall and contains the refrigerator and all the cupboards and drawers. It also integrates a cleaning room and storage pantry in such a way that the kitchen space remains perfectly clear.

When lit up from the inside, the yellow panels transmit a warm, fresh light. The surface of the peninsula that delineates the space contains the kitchen as well as the wash area and in its lower section also integrates the oven, washing machine, and storage space for utensils. All this makes this kitchen a highly functional space, where order comes without effort.

The central module's generous dimensions allow the other side to be used as a bar/lounge for relaxation, which acts as a filter to the adjacent areas. In a space where horizontal lines dominate, the ventilation hood stands out, built from stainless steel like the work surface and descending like a pillar from the ceiling.

The side wall accommodates a horizontal cabinet and a shelf that displays elements, which give emphasis to the identity of this space.

GREENWICH 497/6B APARTMENT

Architect: Winka Dubbledam/Archi-tectonics Photos: © Floto & Warner

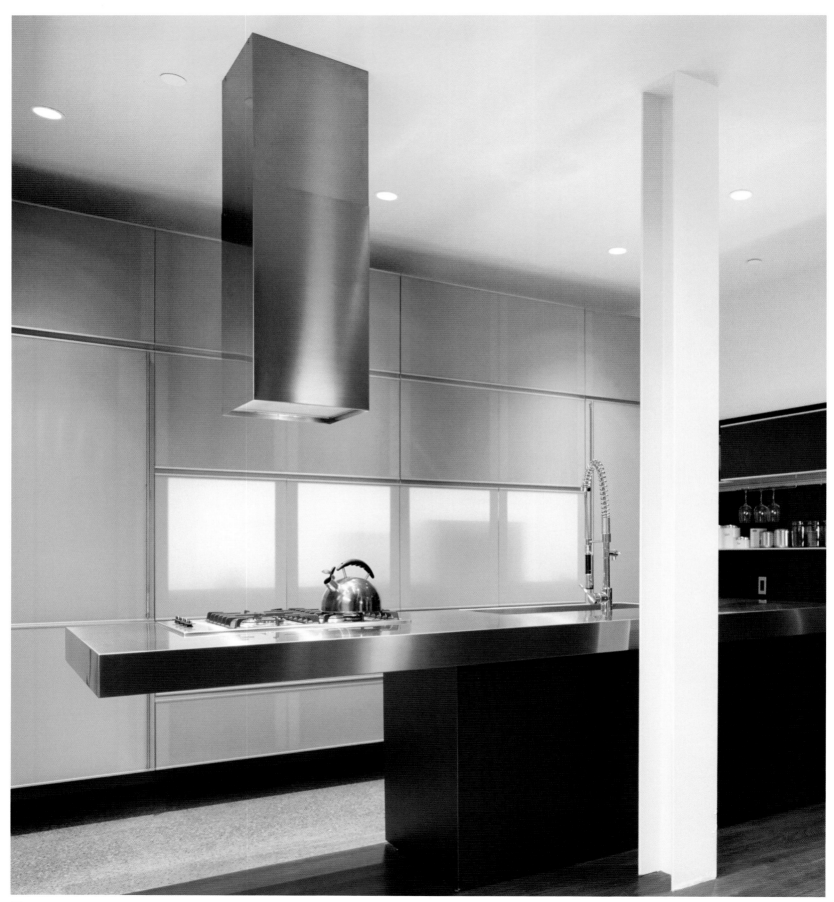

This building was built in the 1930s by architect and engineer Sir Owen Williams as a warehouse for the De Havilland aviation company. In 1998, it was transformed into forty-one basic lofts, preserving the modernist elements that gave its character in such a way that each owner was able to design his interior according to his needs.

The kitchen was positioned to be a reception space and benefited from the position of the beams. The height of the ceiling allowed for the creation of a half upper floor, and it was decided to integrate the kitchen in the space formed beneath the platform. This way, the ceiling of the kitchen is also the floor of the raised level, emphasizing the distinctive homogeneity of this project. Chance played an important role in this project, because large boards of African walnut—which were acquired for the renovation of the interior of the Royal Opera House but were later rejected due to certain defects—could be bought at a price that ordinarily would have been way beyond the budget. Because there was so much wood available, the structure of the raised floor could be made as well as all the furniture coverings of the kitchen, including the refrigerator, which made use of the stairwell. Boards with the same dimensions, although thinner, were used to cover the floor, although before laying them, they were left to adapt to the conditions of the floor to take on their definitive state. Finally, one of the thicker boards was used as a large table, which delimits the kitchen space. From the living area, the balance created by the two parallel tables of equal thickness can be appreciated.

LOFT IN DE HAVILLAND STUDIOS

Architect: McDowell & Benedetti Photos: © Jordi Miralles

The stairwell has been used to accommodate the refrigerator, which, along with the other electrical appliances, is covered in walnut wood forming a uniform surface.

The contrast between the cold stainless steel and warm walnut wood is a spectacular fusion of organic beauty and elegant functionality. The steel of the work surfaces attracts all the light. Thus the kitchen instead of being dark becomes a light and attractive space.

In this bright and open apartment, there are no conventional walls separating the rooms, but the various sections are opened or closed by means of the existing sculptures that substantially shape the living space.

In a simple, yet extraordinary way, one of these five sculptures serves as the kitchen worktop. Other cupboards or cooking utensils are located inside the next sculpture that separates the kitchen from the bedroom behind. This wall-like sculpture has an integrated sliding door ensuring flexibility by allowing a separation or combination of the bedrooms and the cooking and living areas.

This special architectural feature—the separation of rooms by means of sculptures instead of walls—perfectly connects the different living areas of the apartment, visually and physically highlighting the kitchen in an important and central position.

Inside the apartment, the light plays a key role with white sculptures reflecting the light and creating gaps where the light can penetrate freely as to illuminate the space. This turns the entire apartment into a very bright and friendly place but also into an elegant one. It appears like a genuine piece of art perfused with light.

FIVE SCULPTURES

Architect: Gus Wüstemann Photos: © Bruno Helbling

In this apartment, situated in a building from the beginning of the twentieth century, the original structure and finishes fuse with the new modules and the modern divisions of space. The kitchen forms part of the living room, though it is possible to separate it with a blind.

The large windows provide the interior with a large amount of light, giving more freedom to the choice of colors and materials. Here, the contrasts are established between modules and white walls and the floor and some matt wooden surfaces.

The kitchen is the actual center of these pavilions that combine living, dining, and cooking areas.

Like the rest of the house, this space is kept in a natural and rustic style radiating a sense of coziness and warmth.

Different types of wood were used for the design. An exceptional feature is the boat-shaped wooden table that reflects the shape of both the roof and the slopes surrounding the house. The dark tabletop stands out and immediately catches the visitor's eye.

The kitchen has additional functions that go beyond the classical principles, such as the air-conditioning that is installed inside and above the cabinetry. Besides, there is a small home office behind the cabinets that is separated from the rest of the room.

DOWNING RESIDENCE

Architect: Ibarra Rosano Design Architects Photos: © Bill Timmerman

With this kitchen design, the architects from Hecker, Phelan & Guthrie show how to efficiently use the space of an elongated kitchen.

The horizontal concept allows for the sink, the cooktop, the dishwasher, the dining table, and the counter to be combined in one single row. The rectangular space of the kitchen unit does not touch the wall and is accessible from all sides, perfectly occupying the available space and conveying a sense of openness and generosity.

The white, black, red, and silver colors seem to further enlarge and brighten up the space and they give it a modern and innovative character. All in all, the design is dominated by a daring combination of cool materials and bright and friendly colors giving the kitchen a very individual touch. Furthermore, the distinctive design of the ventilation hood enhances this impression.

A dining table is attached to both ends of the counter, one of them connecting to the remaining living space. Thanks to its size and the incidence of light, this table may be used as both a dining table and a desk. In the laterals at the other end of the room, you can find the cupboards that may be used for storing kitchen utensils.

APARTMENT IN MELBOURNE

Architect: Hecker, Phelan & Guthrie Photos: © Shania Shegedyn

White, black, and red preside over this cheerful kitchen, whose finishes have been calculated down to the last detail. The light enters from different angles of the room, and the vegetation penetrates the interior through large doors and windows that give access to the terrace.

The central island, which is curved to make optimal use of the space, integrates functions for both cooking and relaxing. The elegant ceiling fixture gives a warm light at night. The oval shape of the ventilation hood stands out, indicating the work area.

This house, situated to the north of Baviera, has been designed to have a dual use as a home and as a display space. The central idea of the project was therefore to create a multipurpose space that could accommodate these two functions simultaneously. Due to the area's lush, thick vegetation, the house has been opened towards the north and west by way of large windows.

The main space is a single unit, which encompasses the kitchen, living room, and dining area, all of which are closely linked to the outside through these openings. A strong light penetrates the space affording beautiful views of the rest area created in the garden. As well as glass, two other sober materials have been used to construct the interior: concrete for the walls and kitchen surfaces and wood for the floor. The space, the light, and the garden were able to combine with these harsh forms. The modules, cupboards, and drawers of the kitchen are hidden in the peninsula, which integrates the cooktop and sink in the interior wall, hidden from view from the living space. When needed, a series of foldable panels hide the kitchen and the shelves for the stereo and television, making the walls of the living/dining room a compact surface. Only the fireplace is left in view—a square, open cavity of concrete in front of which is the sofa.

The result is a daring, functional, and versatile space.

KAUFMANN HOUSE

Architect: Bembé-Dellinger Photos: © Stefan Müller

Cooking, dining, and living in one single room—this was the concept for this spacious modern house.

As hospitality plays an important role for the two architect homeowners, this spacious kitchen was built to directly connect to the bright and friendly dining room that opens to the garden in summer time. The key element of the cooking area is the large kitchen island in its center. It allows for several people to prepare food together in the same place and to eat their meal there as well. Thus the kitchen is the general meeting spot of the house and brings together both family and visitors at its very center.

The use of the key materials—oak combined with stainless steel—creates a cozy atmosphere that is enhanced by the wide-angled incidence of light.

KERRY MILLETT'S HOUSE

Designer: **John Harvey Design** Photos: © Carlos Domínguez

The large surface area of this kitchen/dining area, the result of joining four separate units, allows different openings to the outside by way of the four sides, allowing the entry of light and vegetation. The result is a multipurpose space, which is cozy, practical, and comfortable.

From the outside, the arbor appears as a floating unit, which in summer can be totally opened to the outside, connecting the kitchen with the garden. A foosball table, possible thanks to the generous space, alludes to family reunions where each member can do as he/she pleases.

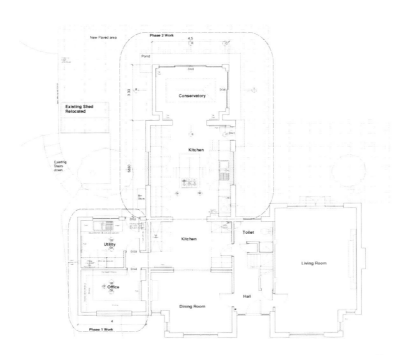

Plan

This elongated kitchen is situated in a narrow corridor and opens to the various areas of the house. On one side, it opens to a covered BBQ-area that can be used in all weather, and on the other side, it opens to the living room where the dining area is located as well. The flexible table was designed especially for the narrow spaces of the building and may be extended or retracted as required. The sloping alignment of the table catches the eye and gives the room a vibrant and dynamic quality. Moreover, it forms a contrast to the strikingly horizontal alignment of the entire room. Another interesting feature of the table is the incorporation of a twenty-four bottle winerack.

At the front, the kitchen opens to the inner courtyard. The access to the outside area is via sliding doors that can be opened completely and, consequently, convey a sense of openness even though the kitchen is designed as a separate space.

BONDI JUNCTION RESIDENCE

Architect: David Boyle Photos: © Murray Fredericks

The kitchen of this loft high above the New York is an oasis in the midst of urban turmoil. The square self-contained kitchen is situated at the center of the living space between the dining and living areas. It enhances the view to all sides and is equipped with two entries on two sides granting access.

The overall ambience is very calming and pleasant despite the colourful and dainty style of the design. The clients are real wine connoisseurs and asked for a nature-related design, which was carried out in a very harmonious way through a range of colors as well as with materials like wood and marble. Abstract patterns and images bear further creative references to viniculture. The possibility of planting herbs and flowers in front of the sink animates the entire space and accentuates the close contact with nature. Consequently, the light, materials, and colors emphasize the unique visual and emotional experience of this highly personalized loft.

ASTOR PLACE PENTHOUSE LOFT

Architect: Cha & Innerhofer Architecture + Design Photos: © Dao Lou Zha

Small but highly functional, this New York kitchen is part of a cell that was installed in place of walls to maximize daylight and space.

The outer area comprises the kitchen and opens to the dining and living spaces, whereas the inner area includes a bathroom and a small workspace, located between the living room and the bathroom. The cell does not touch the ceiling and may be opened or closed by means of sliding doors.

Light colored eco-friendly materials such as wood and glass were used for the kitchen. They harmonize with the rest of the apartment and create a cozy atmosphere. The wooden kitchen counter performs different functions thus perfectly connecting the various spaces: in the kitchen, it may be used as a worktop, in the living area, it can serve as a bar or as part of the entry area, it can be used for storage.

The combination of several details ensures a unique experience. The counter, for instance, contains a wine cabinet; a black pillar with blackboard coating creates a touch of personality and vividness. At the end of the kitchen, is another unique feature: a cupboard with sliding doors that open or close the passage to the living room and the sleeping area. It also contains additional storage space.

PEKARSKY APARTMENT

Architect: Cho Slade Architecture   Photos: © Jordi Miralles

The concept of this compact kitchen is best characterized as functional and urban, and the unique and modern style of its form and color make it the eye-catching centerpiece of the house. The cooking area, located underneath the mezzanine and the stairs, has an open plan to the entire living space thus making efficient use of the restricted space. The microwave is incorporated in the construction of the stairs and offers storage space in the built-in cupboards. The holders on the wall can be used for storing additional kitchen equipment and cutlery. This concept has a space-saving effect and equally bestows a sense of personality and vividness to the kitchen. The multifunctional worktop contributes to the space-saving character: due to its dimension and the elevated glass top, it can also be used as a bar or dining table and connects both the cooking and living areas.

LOFT RIO

Architect: Peanutz Architekten Photos: © Thomas Bruns

This half-open kitchen area with its offbeat architecture differs substantially from a classic kitchen. It is located at the heart of this Spanish country house, inside a 4.59-ft-high (1.4 meter) module. This allows for daylight illuminatation of the kitchen from all sides along with an unobstructed view. Furthermore, all kitchen appliances are stored out of sight and do not affect the elegant and pure impression of the environment.

The outer part of the module is equipped with bookshelves, whereas the inside is divided into two areas. Apart from the kitchen, there is also a dining room and a home office separated by a bar area.
The module is surrounded by the living room and a corridor that leads to the private rooms. The dominant colors are black and white, which creates an elegant and balanced atmosphere in the kitchen and throughout the entire environment.

CALVET HOUSE

Architect: Francesc Rifé Photos: © Eugeni Pons

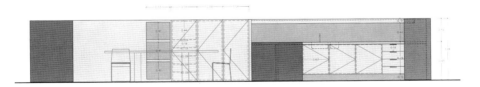

Section

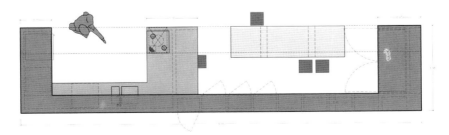

Plan

This unique kitchen is the result of an extension to an old English Victorian house.

In the course of its construction, the architect created the kitchen in the true sense of the word. The dining and cooking areas can be opened directly from the outside by sliding doors, conveying a sense of freedom and complete openness and providing a new access to the garden. The space extends to the outside area dissolving the boundaries between inside and outside. Additionally, daylight can penetrate from above.

The actual cooking area consists of a kitchen island and an additional kitchen range on the outside wall providing space for further storage. The kitchen island serves as a counter and houses the sink. The dining area is located directly behind it and may also be shifted to the terrace.

SEMIDETACHED TUNBRIDGE WELLS

Architect: William Tozer Photos: ceded by William Tozer

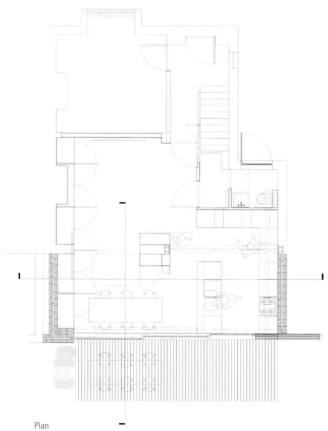

Plan

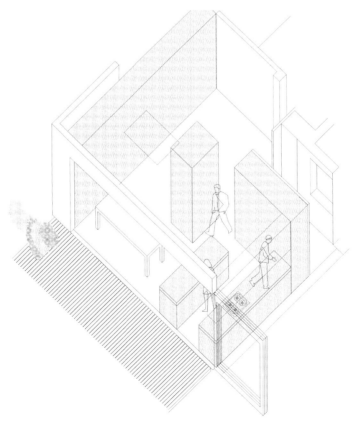

Perspective

SECOND FLOOR

FIRST FLOOR

GROUND FLOOR

Elevation

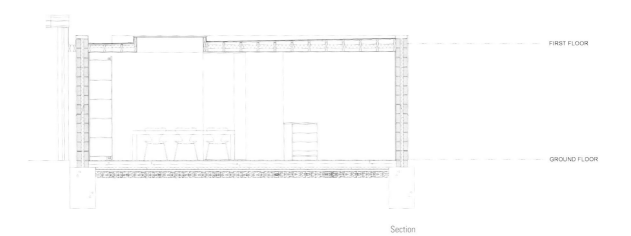

FIRST FLOOR

GROUND FLOOR

Section

This house was totally transformed from an original building from the 1920s. Sited at a higher elavation, there is a spectacular view of the city's skyline from the terrace. The kitchen is situated on the upper floor, and its completely glass walls make it a light box, which at the same time gives light to the central part of the adjacent lounge area.

The furniture, in black and white, except for the large red cupboard situated by the terrace, has been chosen and arranged to facilitate cleaning and tidy-ing up tasks, which are highly necessary in such confined space. The lower modules have no handles, which along with the polished wooden floor, high-lights the effect of cleanliness and distinctive shine of this kitchen.

On the exterior, overhanging screens protect the interior from excessive light. Also discreet sliding panels can hide the kitchen and the terrace from view of the neighboring houses. This way, the terrace space is added to the kitchen extending it and affording it a living space if desired.

RESIDENCE IN COLLINGWOOD

Architect: David Luck Photos: © Shania Shegedyn

The wall that connects the kitchen with the living room has been opened, extending the view to the exterior and increasing the interaction between the two spaces. The orientation increases the functionality because it receives a large amount of natural light throughout most of the day.

The polished wooden floor generates a contrast with the matt surfaces of the modules of this compact kitchen, although it all helps to increase the sensation of simplicity and tidiness. The access to the terrace compensates efficiently for the reduced dimensions.

The work on this house has been done in close collaboration with the owners, who wanted an uncluttered and warm home, which would also, in some way, reflect the Australian spirit. A flexible, integrated space was designed where the kitchen and the living room would communicate freely with the exterior. The open fireplace on the wall opposite the kitchen is an example of the synthesis of warmth and modernity that this house combines.

The kitchen is a large space, as were the clients' needs who wanted a comfortable and functional area, given the amount of time they would spend here. At the same time, they set an aesthetical criteria in accordance with its close proximity to the living room. The working surfaces have great depth to be able to handle large utensils and are finished in stainless steel. A tall single-piece skirting board protects the adjacent wall and facilitates clean-ing. The island that integrates the work area and the storage is facing outwards like an illuminated acrylic cube, which gives the living area personality. The open shelving simplifies access to the utensils and lends character to this area of clean lines. The ceiling of the kitchen is fitted with various lines of built-in lights, which offer a soft and efficient light. The pantry, situated on one side, has a sliding door, which hides it whenever direct access is not required. The flooring is made of polished, insulated cement with the aggregate left in view, giving a mineral quality.

In order to take full advantage of the physical and atmospherical conditions of the area, priority has been given to the concept of intelligent use of energy: the house has tanks that collect rainwater and solar panels on the roof generate electricity and return it to the city's electrical grid.

CASTAN HOUSE

Architect: Robert Grodski Architects   Photos: © John Gollings

This project of architect Greg Gong reveals a very particular style of openness. After the complete renovation of the rear part of the house, the kitchen was relocated to the front of the building in order to take advantage of the existing space beside the entrance and increase the living space. The aim was to maintain the existing structure and the open concept of the veranda. The thin blinds were installed to protect privacy without sacrificing daylighting. Several architectural features turn this kitchen into a unique statement. The one-piece counter is set off against the glazed wall and therefore almost seems to float in space. Additional cupboards were discreetlyw incorporated into the existing wall in order to perserve space.

A dining corner is located in the front part of the kitchen, right next to the entrance of the building. It is well concealed by a transparent glass table and emphasizes the open character of the kitchen.

KOOYONG ROAD HOUSE

Architect: Greg Gong Photos: © John Gollings

In this aesthetically modest kitchen, use of space is maximized with large built-in cupboards situated along the walls that conceal all the utensils.

Translucent screens over the large front window restrict views of the kitchen from passersby, generating intimacy. In the dining area, which reaches the terrace thanks to the creation of a glass box, the vegetation can be appreciated through the side window.

At night, spots hidden behind furniture elements highlight the clean volumes of the whole set while creating different atmospheres.

The diversity of materials is one of the outstanding elements. Glossy white surfaces combind with glass and steel have been used extensively to effectively contrast with the warm red brick of the original façade.

Cheerful, practical, and colorful, this open kitchen projects from a recess into the workspace of the client, a Berlin artist. It is a hybrid between a piece of kitchen furniture and a workbench, featuring an incorporated sink at its overhanging end.

The kitchen combines two functions and saves a lot of space in the process. Having an elongated form, the kitchen makes the most of the limited space.

The concrete surface combines all the essential appliances and cupboards and forms the sink and washbasin. Turquoise mosaic tiles on the wall and the floor provide a colorful environment and have a vibrant effect. A large window allows ample daylight into the kitchen and creates a friendly environment. Furthermore, the design features translucent walls made of industrial glass separating the kitchen from the bathroom.

HOUSE IN THE SOUTH OF BERLIN

Architect: Peanutz Architekten Photos: © Stefan Meyer

This industrial-style kitchen shows a combination of elegant, modern, and innovative design.

It consists of three elements sharing a generous space. Cupboards on the two existing walls can be used for storing food, utensils, and electrical appliances. A large corner combination is placed in the middle of the room connecting the worktop with the dining table. The two areas are differentiated through the contrasting materials of steel and wood, and in combination with the extraordinary L-shape, they turn this island into a very interesting and practical constellation. The ventilation hood in a genuine cafeteria kitchen's style reaches from the wall and stretches along half of the ceiling. The sink is designed accordingly.

On one side, the kitchen opens to the garden via large glass doors, on the other side it connects visually to the living area through the staircase. Consequently, there is always plenty of daylight creating a friendly and cozy atmosphere.

VILLA DE JONG

Architect: Thijs Asselbergs/Architectuur Centrale Photos: © Luuk Kramer

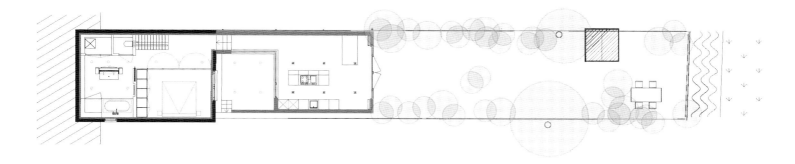

Plan

This extraordinary apartment features a stylized glacier that flows through the entire space and primarily serves as a physical connection to both the terrace and the incidence of light. At the heart of the loft, the glacier directly merges with the kitchen. Thus the glacier and the adjacent kitchen can be regarded as the communicative center of the apartment. The result is a podium from which the rest of the apartment can be observed while allowing the direct sunlight full access.

The predominantly white palette creates an interior that is reminiscent of a frozen lake at the end of a snowy mountain ridge. The kitchen is an integral part of this architectural landscape and at the same time, it forms the center of it. In order not to disrupt this impression, all electronic devices have been well concealed. In this way, the kitchen integrates itself into spaces that are fundamentally comprised of straight horizontal and vertical lines.

GLACIER

Architect: Gus Wüstemann Photos: © Bruno Helbling

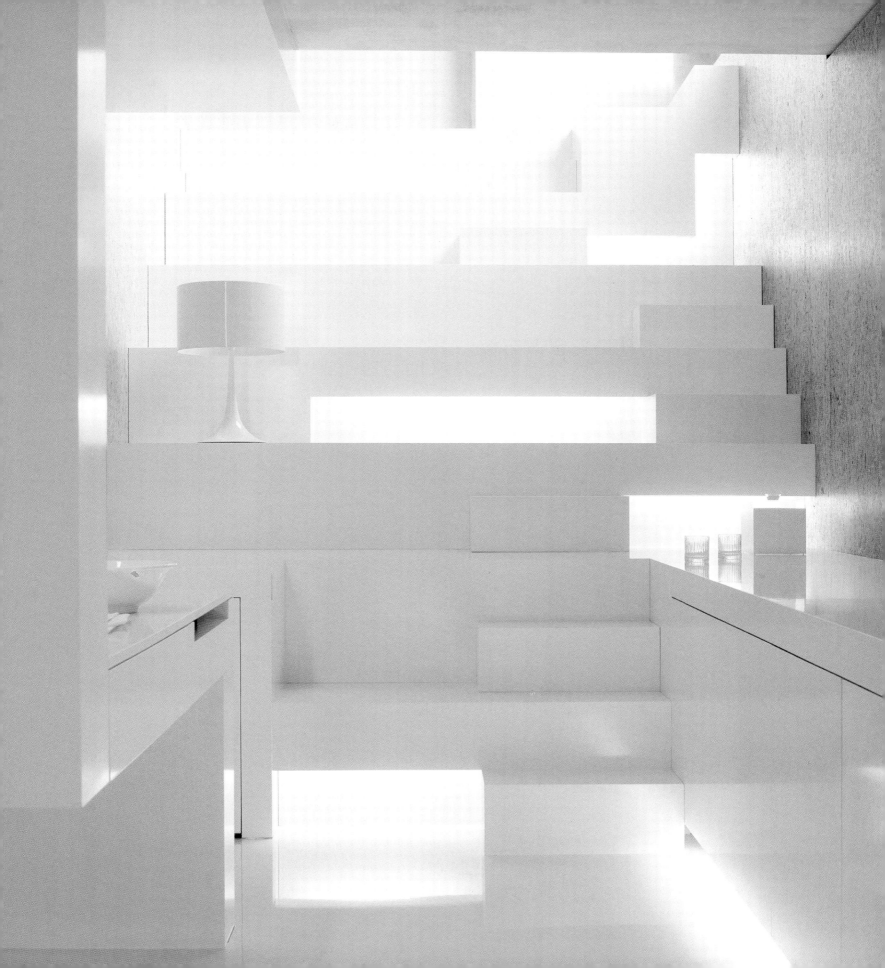

In front of the kitchen, the table, made from one piece of plastic, can be converted into a desk or used as a dining table. The curved forms of both the table and the Panton chairs contrast with the lines of the kitchen.

The immaculate white palette of this apartment is further enhanced in the kitchen area thanks to a system of lights and a combination of volumes that emphasize the igloo-like feeling of the space.

Situated on the top floor of a building in the center of Milan is this open-plan loft apartment, with its L-shaped central body. The vertebrate axis of this form is the dining area, established as an intersection between the kitchen and the living area. All the flooring has been covered in wood, except in the kitchen, where the blue mosaic spreads around the floor and walls, creating a cube, set apart from the other spaces. A long modular furnishing occupies the length of the back wall, integrating some of the appliances and becoming a sideboard when it reaches the dining area. Given the great height of the ceilings, a mezzanine was built that allows natural light to easily reach the ground floor. The kitchen has been positioned just beneath a skylight and receives a large amount of natural light. The adjacent wall that runs around the living and dining room, has been painted red to lend vivacity to this light space of simple lines and smart finishes.

LOFT IN MILAN

Architect: Carlo Colombo   Photos: © Santi Caleca

Located right next to the main entrance of a modern Melbourne loft, this unconventional kitchen creates an indelible first impression and welcomes every visitor by reflecting the philosophy of the entire apartment. The straight, simple lines and straightforward, modern design demonstrate this kitchen's unique and elegant character. Not only the kitchen, but the entire space is dominated by the color white, radiating a touch of coldness but also providing a predominantly clean and elegant atmosphere.

The ventilation hood, reminiscent of a design masterpiece, features built-in illumination—an important feature given that the hood extends over the entire length of the work area.

WEST MELBOURNE HOUSE

Architect: Greg Gong Photos: © John Gollings

One of the most striking aspects of this restoration is the strong contrast between the different materials used, which the lighting maximizes. A black concrete work island proves to be a strong contrast in this light space of otherwise shiny surfaces.

In the living area, horizontal lines dominate. The black-and-white scheme is terminated by a vivid yellow coffee table. The glow of the fireplace with its sheet-stell mantel, effectively complements the table's yellow tone.

This kitchen is part of a spacious and highly impressive Milan loft featuring a simple yet elegant and extraordinary interior design.
The cooking area is located behind one of the rear corners of the loft and is divided into three parts: one traditional kitchen range and two steel carts that can be used for storage or as work surfaces and that can be placed wherever needed. Altogether, the kitchen has a rather simple furnishing leaving plenty of space for modifications.

Black is the basic color of the kitchen, providing an elegant accent and perfectly blending with the dark pile structure in the style of a Japanese temple. Colorful elements of the room form a contrast to this dark environment: such as the colorful lamps or the blue walls, both ensuring a balanced and friendly atmosphere.
Altogether, the place is dominated by its spacious dimension and its utmost flexibility, giving the apartment its unique character.

BEACH HOUSE IN MILAN

Architect: Johanna Grawunder Photos: © Santi Caleca

Moving away from more conventional proposals, transitory elements such as this picnic table have been used, which fuses the terrace with the interior, or the modules on wheels, which is, in fact, office furniture. The whole setup, with its simplicity, accentuates the importance of details.

The chromatic combination has been the basis on which this project has been created. The concrete features, painted in black, enhance the light colors of the walls and the vivid details. The abundant natural light has allowed for freedom when choosing the interior lighting.

As generosity and openness play an important role for the owner of this villa situated on a hill overlooking Lake Zurich, it was the architect's task to transform this concept architecturally. The result is a succession of rooms full of suspense, equipped with a scarce number of walls and featuring broad passages.

The kitchen is part of this environment and has an independent structure, yet it opens to the other parts and is easily accessible from all sides. Similar to an enfilade, the place ranges from the entrance to the kitchen continuing via the living and dining room all the way through the library and back again to the entry area. Although the various rooms are connected with each other in a very open way, the rooms were intended to retain their specific character, which was ensured by the varying choice of material and illumination.

The friendly cooking area extends into the living room like a body of fitted furniture. In front of the window, this body turns into a bench similar to the seats that are incorporated into the walls of palaces and castles. Another remarkable feature is the illumination that is integrated all along the body, illuminating the wall and the counter.

Thanks to these details, this white kitchen is extraordinary notwithstanding the simplicity of its design.

MÖHR'S HOUSE

Architect: Philippe Stuebi Architekten Photos: © Andreas Ilg

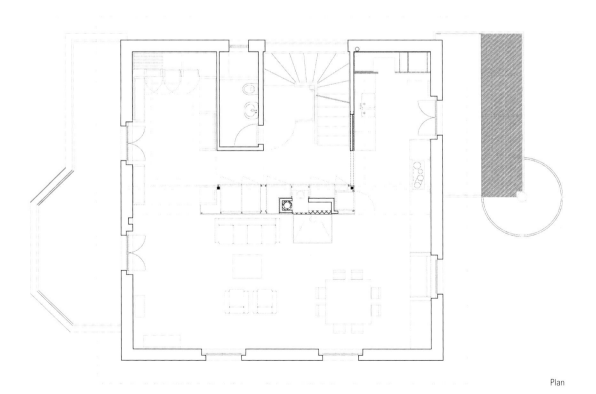

Plan

This kitchen forms the center of a spacious Berlin loft, and its simple and extraordinary shapes express an extremely modern style. The ventilation hood extends over the entire counter and performs additional functions serving as a source of light and offering additional storage space for dishes and various kitchen utensils. This space-saving design perfectly combines aesthetics and functionality.

The kitchen is open on three sides eliminating the boundaries between the different living areas and embracing the bar as well as the cooking and dining space. There is also a small library behind the bar that can be used while enjoying a meal. The central location of this kitchen offers a special meeting space and unites the different living spaces at the heart of the apartment.

LOFT BEVERLY HILLS

Architect: Peanutz Architekten Photos: © Thomas Bruns

Despite the simplicity and the inconspicuousness of its design, this kitchen consisting of an island and a wall cupboard has a exceptional character. The entirely black work island forms a contrast to the bright furniture and therefore functions as the central focus of the entire room. Additionally, it blends with the minimalist look of the house, mostly characterised by straight lines and unobtrusive forms. Due to its entirely flat surface, the kitchen island is not at all reminiscent of a classic kitchen range. Accord-ingly, the cupboards seem to incorporate the appliances and almost entire-ly conceal them. The cooking area is located at the edge of the living room, underneath the stairs that emerge right at the heart of the room and divide the front part of the kitchen at its center. The ascending element creates a roof over the kitchen and forms an interesting contrast to the horizontal lines dominating the other parts of the space.

K80 HOUSE

Architect: BO 6 Architectenbureau Photos: © Luuk Kramer

The island in the work space of the kitchen is the only module in this area. It was therefore possible to successfully position it under the stairs that lead to the next floor. The oval wall separates the bedroom from the kitchen and living area and integrates the bathrooms.

With the intent of increasing space, the relief of the surfaces has been reduced as much as possible in order to obtain a polished and continual effect. The long continual wall of cupboards runs around the entire space from the kitchen to the bedroom, changing function as it changes area.

This extraordinary cooking area at the far end of a modern living room appears like a veritable piece of art than a mere kitchen. In this exceptional design, the architect combines aesthetics with functionality and creates a balanced modern-style kitchen. The kitchen is divided into two areas. The main area is located directly within the living area, the smaller one inside an extension that connects to the garden area. Both the sink and the dishwasher are placed in this area where they remain out of sight. Other appliances and cupboards are concealed behind the rear wall of the kitchen's inner area. The symmetrical counter stands out visually and represents a key element of the cooking area. It is made out of brightly colored wood and with its elegance and simplicity, it blends perfectly with the style of the living area. Conversely, the turquoise ventilation hood presents a very playful design that conveys a vibrant quality to the space.

MALVERN HOUSE

Architect: Greg Gong Photos: © John Gollings

It is not only the location or the spectacular sea view that makes the kitchen of this Japanese guesthouse so impressive, but also its sublime architecture.

In this design, several levels are held together by the same horizontal surfaces: consequently, an elevated counter at one level transisitions to a low table at another level.

The colors perfectly blend with the environment. The space is dominated by a palette of blue, brown, red, and white that create a maritime flair and freshness.

The huge counter is a very prominent feature of the room. However, electric appliances are stored on the sides so as to not interupt the view or the minimalist design.

N GUESTHOUSE

Architect: Takao Shiotsuka Atelier Photos: © Kaori Ichikawa

This modern, luxurious, and elegant kitchen opens both to the interior of the house as well as extending outside towards the garden. This structural feature reflects the client's desire to be able to cook outside and to benefit more from the direct contact with the garden. This creative design turns the kitchen into the meeting place of the house and makes it the center of all social activity. During nice weather, the meal preparation can be done in the outside kitchen, which is accessed via a sliding door. In poor weather, the client still has a spectacular view of the garden and the water basin while inside.

GEORGIAN TERRACE

Architect: F2 Architects Photos: © Shania Shegedyn

There is great homogeneity between the interior and exterior of this home, where straight lines, the texture of the materials, and the use of water transmit calm and stillness. Using the depth of the window frame, the living area is protected from excessive light.

The large glass surfaces give the kitchen area continuity, so that the interior work area continues towards the exterior as a single unit. In the space with free access to the terrace, an informal living and dining area can be improvised.

The modern open kitchen of this New York loft welcomes visitors at the entrance of the apartment that belongs to a photographer couple. This coherent living space has no boundaries; therefore rooms merge into one another and perform various functions. The dining area is not only intended for dining, but it can also be used for working. Additionally, there is a special working area at the rear of the loft, which also serves as a guest room.

A mixture of different materials and colors creates a vibrant atmosphere that ensures an extremely personal and unique style. The dark colors of the kitchen contrast with the rest of the apartment, in particular with the wooden table that is placed in front of it, in the center of the loft. This table turns the cooking and dining area into the meeting place of the entire apartment.

NO-HO LOFT

Architect: Slade Architects Photos: © Jordi Miralles

Plan

When dining or cooking in this kitchen designed by architect William Tozer, the owners and their visitors can directly experience the outdoors.

The new annex is equipped with glazed sliding doors that completely open to provide full access to the terrace and garden.

The cooking area consists only of two parts, an inconspicuous kitchen unit and a simple kitchen island. From all sides you can enjoy the magnificent view and the open atmosphere. Even from above, light and air penetrate the space and increase the sense of freedom and infinity. Between the cooking area and the terrace, there is enough space for the large dining table that can easily be placed on the terrace as needed.

All in all, the prevailing character of white and bright colors creates a modern and pure atmosphere that contrasts with nature itself. However, the bright wooden floor blending into the dark-toned terrace floor creates a certain connection to the outside area and enhances the space's cozy atmosphere.

OPEN END

Architect: William Tozer Photos: ceded by William Tozer

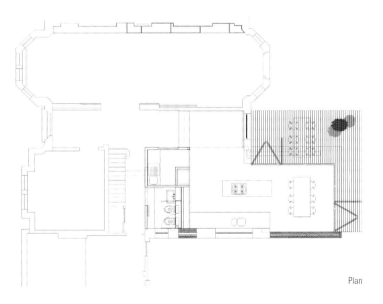

Plan

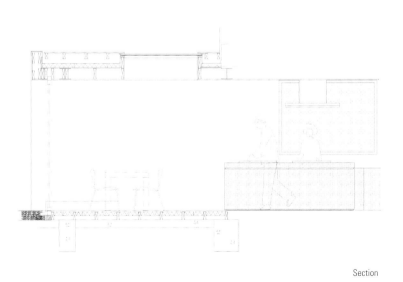

Section

The owner's desire to live in an open and modern space is reflected by the flexibility of this space that can be completely opened to the adjacent living spaces. The kitchen is located within the living and dining spaces and can be opened to the study by a sliding door.

The materials used for this design are combined in a very sophisticated way so as to redefine modernity and aesthetics. Moreover, straight lines and minimalist traits characterize the room, whereas the dining room is furnished in a rather playful way. The different contrasts are the actual protagonists of this loft. The design shows us a kitchen that at a first glance does not attract a lot of attention, yet it is very exclusive. This is proven by the sophisticated bar stools that fit perfectly underneath the counter and were especially designed for the location.

VAN BREESTRAAT

Architect: Marc Prosman Architecten, John Pawson Photos: © Christian Richters

The kitchen, designed by architect John Pawson, is a well-defined space, although the length of the work module that stretches to the dining area enhances its open nature. Two simple wooden cubes are used as stools.

The texture of the stone, steel, marble, and glass is highlighted thanks to the straight lines and clean cuts. In the adjacent dining area, the feet of the columns and bronze table create a beautiful contrast with this simplicity.

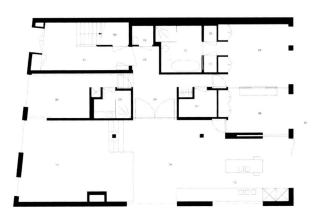

Before situation ground floor

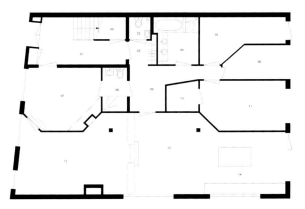

After situation ground floor

This kitchen, located at the end of the open living area, blends into the prevailing style of the apartment. The space is dominated by colors that are used in the furnishings as well as in the curtains, which perserves the privacy of the kitchen.

The dining area, located in front of the kitchen unit, closely connects to the living room. The seemless unity of kitchen, dining and living areas is highlighted by the illumination, another significant element of this design.

This art nouveau apartment is divided into two main areas—a night zone and a day zone. The day zone consist of a living and dining room as well as the kitchen area. The simple white design of this unit features a white frame both separating and dividing the areas. The transparent wall also isolates any cooking odors from the living room area.

The kitchen in the rear has a modest design and fades from the spotlight.

PINK HOUSE

Architect: **Filippo Bombace** Photos: © **Luigi Filetici**

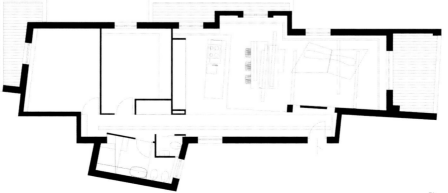

Plan

This kitchen combines the requirements of a contemporary and functional kitchen with the desire to create an individual space that reflects the personality and lifestyle of the client, a businesswoman and art collector.
The various ways of utilizing and combining the space define the actual shape of this kitchen.
The kitchen's curve is made out of a material that can be used in many different ways. Laminated plastic plates curl around the walls like ribbons, unfolding from the worktop into a sink and then transforming into a dining table. This dynamic curve extends like a huge clamp embracing much more than the actual space reserved for the counter. As a result, it unites the cooking and dining spaces. The kitchen is located right at the entrance and takes perfect advantage of the space so as to fully unite it. With the sculptural character, the kitchen snuggles up around the fittings making use of the existing elements thus attributing a new meaning to the space.

RESIDENCE IN VIENNA

Architect: Lena Schacherer, Ivo Dolezalek Photos: © Karoline Mayer

Plan

The owner of this kitchen is a fashion designer who is extremely demanding when it comes to interior design. The unusual materials were chosen according to his preferences and the different living areas have been designed to harmonize perfectly. Certain materials can be found throughout the entire house. When entering the place, you already see the glazed kitchen wall—a combination of a steel frame and glass—and similar structures can be found in both the foyer and the bathroom. The extraordinary partition walls give the apartment a unique character.

The kitchen is separated by the entrance area through a glazed wall, but it remains open to the main living area. As a result, the view into the kitchen is blurred and kitchen odors can be controlled. At the same time, sufficient daylight can penetrate the space while the open atmosphere of the loft is preserved.

The bar unit on casters can be used for storing kitchen appliances while separating the dining area from the living area. This mobile unit also allows for an open or closed traffic pattern through the kitchen, as needed.

FLATIRON LOFT

Architect: Slade Architects   Photos: © Jordi Miralles

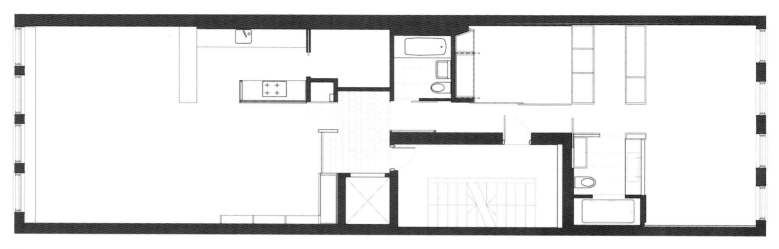

Plan

Because the kitchen is integrated into one of the modules with a translucent wall, the work area automatically acquires a lot of natural light while remaining concealed from the living room. The iron bars allow for hanging some of the bigger utensils.

Putting a module with wheels between the kitchen and dining area seems a very simple idea and yet its functionality is immediately obvious. It separates both rooms and allows movement between them when needed. Industrial elements, which fit into an elegant space.

Directory

Andy Macdonald/Mac-Interactive
94 Cooper Street
Surry Hills NSW 2010, Australia
P: +61 2 9212 3800
F: +61 2 9212 3880
info@mac-interactive.com
www.mac-interactive.com
View Street House, 18–21

Bembé-Dellinger
Im Schloss
86926 Greifenberg, Germany
P: +49 8192 999912
F: +49 8192 996544
mail@bembe-dellinger.de
www.bembe-dellinger.de
Kaufmann House, 60–63

BO 6 Architectenbureau
Wibaustraat, 406
1018DN Amsterdam, The Netherlands
P: +31 20 663 9262
architectenbureau@bo6.nl
K80 House, 146–149

Carlo Colombo
Via Giovanni XXIII, 19
22060 Carimati, Italy
P: +39 031 789 901
F: +39 031 789 902
info@carlocolombo.it
www.carlocolombo.it
Loft in Milan, 122–125

Cha & Innerhofer Architecture + Design
611 Broadway, Suite 540
New York, NY 10012, USA
P: +1 212 477 6957
F: +1 212 353 3286
mail@cha-innerhofer.com
www.cha-innerhofer.com
Astor Place Penthouse Loft, 72–75

Cho Slade Architecture
150 Broadway, 807
New York, NY 10038, USA
P: +1 212 677 6380
F: +1 212 677 6330
info@sladearch.com
www.sladearch.com
Pekarsky Apartment, 76–79

David Boyle
17 Como Parade
Pretty Beach 2257 NSW, Australia
P: +61 4 1966 4836
davidboylearch@bigpond.com
Bondi Junction Residence, 68–71

David Luck
7 Hardy Street
South Yarra 3141VIC, Australia
P/F: +61 3 9867 7509 / +61 3 9677 509
david.luck@bigpond.com
www.users.bigpond.com/david.luck
Residence in Collingwood, 96–99

F2 Architects
Level 1, 450 St. Kilda Road
Melbourne 3004 VIC, Australia
P/F: +61 3 9867 2233
fmarioli@f2architecture.com.au
Georgian Terrace, 158–161

Filippo Bombace
Via Isola del Giglio, 3
00141 Rome, Italy
P/F: +39 0686 898 266
info@filippobombace.com
www.filippobombace.com
Pink House, 174–177

Francesc Rifé
Escoles Pies, 25, bjs.
08017 Barcelona, Spain
P: +34 934 141 208
F: +34 932 412 814
f@rife-design.com
www.rife-design.com
Calvet House, 84–89

Georg Driendl/Driendl Architects
Mariahilferstrasse, 9
1060 Wien, Austria
P: +43 1 585 1868
F: +43 1 585 1869
architect@driendl.at
www.driendl.at
Solar Tube, 26–29

Greg Gong
326 Tooronga Road
Malvern 3146 VIC, Australia
P/F: +61 3 9822 2892 / +61 4 2222 3290
omegagg@ihug.com.au
Kooyong Road House, 104–109
Malvern House, 150–153
West Melbourne House, 126–129

Gus Wüstemann
Gus Wüstemann Zurich
Köchlichstrasse, 15
Ch-8004 Zurich, Switzerland
P: +41 44 295 6016

Gus Wüstemann Barcelona
Rambla de les Flors, 73, 3-2
08002 Barcelona, Spain
P: +34 93 301 14 45
architects@guswustemann.com
www.guswustemann.com
5 Sculptures, 48–51
Glacier, 118–121

Hecker, Phelan & Guthrie
3C/68 Oxford Street
Collingwood VIC 3066, Australia
P: +61 3 9417 0466
F: +61 3 9417 0866
hp@heckerphelan.com.au
http://hpg.net.au
Apartment in Melbourne, 56–59

Ibarra Rosano Design Architects
2849 East Sylvia Street
Tucson, AR 85716, USA
P: +1 520 795 5477
F: +1 520 795 8699
mail@ibarrarosano.com
www.ibarrarosano.com
Downing Residence, 52–55

Johanna Grawunder
Johanna Grawunder San Francisco
53 Rodgers Street
San Francisco, CA 94103, USA

Johanna Grawunder Milan
Via Volta, 10
20121 Milan, Italy
email@grawunder.com
www.grawunder.com
Beach House in Milan, 130–135

John Harvey Design
London, UK
P: +44 208 467 4719
Kerry Millett's House, 64–67

John Pawson
Unit B
70–78 York Way
London N1 9AG, UK
P: +44 207 837 2929
F: +44 207 837 4949
email@johnpawson.com
www.johnpawson.com
Van Breestraat, 170–173

Jonathan Clark Architects
2nd floor, 34–35 Great Sutton Street
London EC1V 0DX, UK
P: +44 207 608 1111
F: +44 207 490 8530
jonathan@jonathanclarkarchitects
www.jonathanclarkarchitects.co.uk
Highgate House, 8–13

Lena Schacherer, Ivo Dolezalek
kathiskuechenkurve@gmx.at
Residence in Vienna, 178–181

Marc Prosman Architecten
Overtoom, 197
1054 HT Amsterdam, The Netherlands
P: +31 20 489 2099
F: +31 20 489 3658
architekten@prosman.nl
www.prosman.nl
Van Breestraat, 170–173

McDowell & Benedetti
68 Rosebery Avenue
London EC1R 4RR, UK
P: +44 207 278 8810
F: +44 207 278 8844
email@mcdowellbenedetti.com
www.mcdowellbenedetti.com
Loft in De Havilland Studios, 44–47

Moneo Brock Studio
C/ Francisco de Asís
Méndez Casariego, 7, bjs.
28002 Madrid, Spain
P: +34 915 638 056
F: +34 915 638 573
contact@moneobrock.com
www.moneobrock.com
Hudson Street Loft, 22–25

Peanutz Architekten
Elke KnöB & Wolfgang Grillitsch
Schlesische Str., 12, 2. Hof, Fabrik, 4. OG
10997 Berlin, Germany
P: +49 3044 379033
F: +49 3044 379010
post@peanutz-architekten.de
www.peanutz-architekten.de
House in the South of Berlin, 110–113
Loft Beverly Hills, 142–145
Loft Rio, 80–83

Philippe Stuebi Architekten
Hardstrasse, 219
CH-8005 Zurich, Switzerland
P: +41 44 440 7777
F: +41 44 440 7779
contact@philippestuebi.ch
www.philippestuebi.ch
Möhr's House, 136–141

Ramon Pintó
Av. Pau Casals, 7, s/a 2
08021 Barcelona, Spain
P: +34 934 141 061
F: +34 934 141 061
ramonpinto@coac.es
House in Cabrera, 30–33

Robert Grodski Architects
127 Wellington Street
Prahran 3181 VIC, Australia
P: +61 3 9525 2655
F: +61 3 9529 5252
grodskiarchitects@bigpond.com
Castan House, 100–103

Safdie Rabines Architects
1101 Washington Place
San Diego, CA 92103, USA
P: +1 619 297 6153
F: +1 619 299 6072
taal@safdierabines.com
ricardo@safdierabines.com
www.safdierabines.com
Lomac Residence (Tree House), 14–17

Scape Architects
Unit 2 Providence Yard
Ezra Street
London E2 7RJ, UK
P: +44 207 012 1244
F: +44 207 012 1255
mail@scape-architects.com
www.scape-architects.com
Chiswick Penthouse Apartment, 34–39

Slade Architects
150 Broadway, 807
New York, NY 10038, USA
P: +1 212 677 6380
F: +1 212 677 6330
info@sladearch.com
www.sladearch.com
Flatiron Loft, 182–187
No-Ho Loft, 162–165

Takao Shiotsuka Atelier
301-4-1-24, Miyako-machi
Oita-shi, 870-0034 Oita, Japan
P: +81 97 538 8828
F: +81 97 538 8829
shio-atl@shio-atl.com
www.shio-atl.com
N Guesthouse, 154–157

Thijs Asselbergs/Architectuur Centrale
Postbus 3056
2001 DB Haarlem, The Netherlands
P: +31 23 534 6109
F: +31 23 531 1210
info@architectuurcentrale.nl
www.architectuurcentrale.nl
Villa de Jong, 114–117

William Tozer
1st floor 33 D'Arblay Street
London W1F 8EU, UK
P: +44 207 734 6055
F: +44 207 437 7775
william.tozer@wtad.co.uk
www.wtad.co.uk
Open End, 166–169
Semidetached Tunbridge Wells, 90–95

Winka Dubbledam/Archi-tectonics
200 Varick Street, 507B
New York, NY 10014, USA
P/F: +1 212 200 0920
wd@archi-tectonics.com
www.archi-tectonics.com
Greenwich 497/6B Apartment, 40–43